ANIMAL
MECHANICALS

Mammals

Tom Jackson

PowerKiDS
press

Published in 2017 by
The Rosen Publishing Group, Inc.
29 East 21st Street, New York, NY 10010

Cataloging-in-Publication Data

Names: Jackson, Tom.
Title: Mammals / Tom Jackson.
Description: New York : PowerKids Press, 2017. | Series: Animal mechanicals | Includes index.
Identifiers: ISBN 9781508150312 (pbk.) | ISBN 9781508150251 (library bound) | ISBN 9781508150138 (6 pack)
Subjects: LCSH: Mammals--Juvenile literature.
Classification: LCC QL706.2 J32 2017 | DDC 599--dc23

For Brown Bear Books Ltd:
Editorial Director: Lindsey Lowe
Editor: Tom Jackson
Children's Publisher: Anne O'Daly
Design Manager: Keith Davis
Designer: Lynne Lennon
Picture Manager: Sophie Mortimer

Picture Credits
T=Top, C=Center, B=Bottom, L=Left, R=Right
Front Cover: 1st swatch, ©Shutterstock/Mixrinho; 2nd swatch, ©Shutterstock/Igorsky; 3rd swatch, ©Shutterstock/worradirek; bat, ©Shutterstock/Rosa Jay; cheetah, ©Shutterstock/Eric Isselee; polar bear, ©Shutterstock/FloridaStock; elephant, ©Shutterstock/alvi / Shutterstock; dolphins, ©Shutterstock/Willyam Bradberry; hoof illustration, ©Shutterstock/ninocka; push pins, ©Shutterstock/Picsfive; lined paper, ©Shutterstock/Yuttasak Jannarong.**Inside:** 1, ©Shutterstock/Mark Beckwith; 4c, ©Dreamstime/Mark Higgins; 4b, ©Shutterstock/K. A. Willis; 5, ©Shutterstock/Four Oaks; 6b, ©Shutterstock/Stuart. G. Porter; 6-7, ©Shutterstock/Mark Beckwith; 7tr, ©Shutterstock/Mezzotint; 8-9, ©Shutterstock/Matt 9122; 9, ©Shutterstock/ Christian Musat; 10, ©Shutterstock/Memorix Photography; 11, ©Shutterstock/Christian Musat; 12b, ©Shutterstock/Rowan S; 12-13, ©Dreamstime/Izanbar; 14-15, ©Shutterstock/Iakor Filimonov; 15tr, ©Shutterstock/Anita Andre; 15c, ©Shutterstock/ Hayati Kayhan; 16-17, ©Shutterstock/Eric Isselee; 17cr, ©Shutterstock/Holly Kuchera; 18cr, ©Shutterstock/S. R. Maglione; 18cl, ©Shutterstock/Tom Tietz; 19tr, ©Shutterstock/Chris Alcock; 19c, ©Shutterstock/S. R. Maglione; 20b, ©Shutterstock/Will Rodrigues; 20-21, ©Shutterstock/Patryk Kosmider; 21tr, ©Thinkstock/Albina Tipyashina; 22-23, ©Shutterstock/Ivan Kuzmin; 23tr, ©Shutterstock/Ivan Kuzmin; 23cr, ©Thinkstock/Vladimir Zaplakhov/iStock; 23br, ©Shutterstock/Andrea Danti; 24, ©Shutterstock/Jonathan Pledher; 24-25, ©Istock Photo/Liz Leyden; 26-27, ©Dreamstime/Brain Magnier; 27, ©Dreamstime/ Vilinecrevette; 28cl, ©Shutterstock/Menno Schaefer; 28bl, ©Shutterstock/Anna Maria Szilagyi; 28cr, ©Shutterstock/Eco Print; 29tl, ©Shutterstock/Tami Freed; 29cr, ©Dreamstime/Satori13; 29bl, ©Shutterstock/Eric Isselee.

Brown Bear Books has made every attempt to contact the copyright holder.
If anyone has any information please contact licensing@brownbearbooks.co.uk

Manufactured in the United States of America
CPSIA Compliance Information: Batch #BS16PK: For Further Information contact Rosen Publishing, New York, New York at 1-800-237-9932

CONTENTS

Mammal Machines

There are some machines that can outpace a speeding car, go without fuel for days, and carry heavier weights than a forklift truck.

These machines are called mammals. An animal body is a living machine. It is equipped with moving parts, sensors, and a power supply, just like any car, aircraft, or earthmover. The mammal design can be adapted for all kinds of jobs: A cheetah accelerates faster than a Ferrari; a bat flies through the dark seeing with sound; and a polar bear can keep warm even when everything around it is frozen.

Monotreme: Echidna

The Three Main Mammal Groups:

MONOTREMES	*	Lay eggs in nest, includes duck-billed platypus and echidnas
MARSUPIALS	*	Give birth to tiny young, which then grow up inside a pouch, includes koalas and kangaroos
PLACENTAL MAMMALS	*	Babies develop inside the mother and are supplied with food and oxygen, includes most mammals

Marsupial: Kangaroo

Mammal Tech Spec

There are around 5,000 different kinds of mammals. They live all over the world, even in the oceans. Mammal bodies are built in different ways to suit the places they live, but they all share three basic characteristics:

* They have hair or fur on the skin at some point in their lives. Even dolphins are born with a few wispy hairs.

* They all keep their bodies at a certain temperature— whatever the conditions are like outside. This is called being "warm-blooded."

* They all feed their young on milk.

Placental Mammal: Elephant

A baby elephant drinks milk from its mother for at least 5 years.

An elephant's trunk is the world's biggest nose.
* Length: 7 ft (2.1 m); weight: 390 lbs (177 kg)

Elephant mothers are pregnant for 22 months, longer than any other mammal.
* Shortest pregnancy: Virginia opossum, 12 days

Cheetah

TOP SPEED

Whether you're designing an animal or a racing car, top speeds need an aerodynamic shape and lightweight components.

FACT FILE

Common name: Cheetah

Length: head and body 43–59 in (109–150 cm); tail 24–33 in (61–84 cm)

Height: 26–37 in (66–94 cm)

Weight: 125 lbs (57 kg)

Color: yellowy brown, with black spots

Where it lives: northern Iran; the Sahel; western, eastern, and central southern Africa

Prey: small and mid-sized mammals including hares and gazelles

Top speed: 70 mph (113 km/h)

Profile

The cheetah is the quickest animal on land. It's a highly specialized sprinter and agile hunter, able to make sudden turns at high speed. Chases are short and less than a minute. The cheetah takes down its prey with a bite to the neck.

FAULT FINDER

A cheetah can only chase its prey for about 600 yards (550 m) and then has to rest and catch its breath.

BIOMIMIC:

A cheetah's claws never fully retract. That gives them extra grip, like the spikes on the bottom of running shoes help athletes push off the track.

Stride length:
25 ft (7.6 m)

Acceleration:
0-60 mph in 3 seconds
* Ferrari Enzo sports car:
0-60 mph in 3.3 seconds

SPEED SYSTEM

HEAD	Small, to reduce air resistance
SPINE	Flexible, to act as a spring for the legs
HEART	Enlarged, to circulate lots of blood
LUNGS	Enlarged, to take in 150 breaths per minute
EYES	Wide, for a wide-angle view
LEGS	Thin, to keep weight low
TAIL	Long, to act as a balance while cornering

Dolphin

When it comes to speeding through the ocean, the dolphin's sleek body components and smooth skin has it covered.

SUPER SWIMMING

Flat tail provides the power by swinging up and down.
Top speed: 22 mph (35 km/h)
* Sailboat: 8 mph (13 km/h)

FACT FILE

Common name: Bottlenose dolphin

Length: 11 ft 9 in (3.6 m)

Weight: 880 lbs (400 kg)

Color: blue-gray, pale underneath and darker on top

Where it lives: oceans worldwide, wherever the water does not freeze in winter

Prey: fish, octopuses, squids, shrimp, and crabs

Predators: tiger sharks, killer whales, and human hunters

Flippers steer through the water. The back fin provides stability.

BIOMIMIC:

A dolphin's flippers are shaped like a wing. The animal steers up and down by swiveling the flippers. Submarines have curved fins called hydroplanes that work in the same way.

Soft, smooth skin cuts down drag (the force of the water pushing against the dolphin).

Profile

Dolphins are hunters. They live in groups called pods and work as a team to herd fish together, making them easier to catch. Dolphins have many small, pointed teeth in their long beak-like mouths. The teeth work like hooks to grab hold of slippery fish and other prey.

SWIMMING SYSTEM

SKIN	Hairless, to make skin super smooth
BUOYANCY	A thick layer of fat under the skin acts like a lifejacket; it helps the dolphin stay afloat
BLOWHOLE	Breathes air in and out through a single nostril on top of its head; it only needs to break the surface to take a breath
SONAR	Uses sound to detect prey; echoes bounce off objects in the water

Giraffe
REACHING HIGH

Reaching up to high places requires a long neck combined with great strength and flexibility. The giraffe's design has it all.

Profile

The giraffe is a leaf eater, and it uses its great height to reach up to the tops of trees, where the freshest leaves grow. It wraps its flexible tongue, which is 18 inches (46 cm) long—and blue!—around twigs and pulls off the leaves. The giraffe's lips are covered in rough bumps that protect them from prickly thorns.

Heartbeat is twice as powerful as a human's to push blood up to the head.

STANDING TALL

The giraffe is the tallest animal in the world. The great height comes from long legs and an even longer neck.

KICK DEFENSE	One kick, strong enough to kill a lion
NECK DEFENSE	Swinging neck to hit threats delivers mighty blow
BLOOD VALVES	Valves close the neck's blood vessels when the giraffe lowers its head; that keeps high-pressure blood from damaging the brain

FAULT FINDER

Giraffes find it hard to sit down so they give birth standing up. The newborn calf plunges 6 feet (1.8 m) to the ground!

The neck is made up of seven bones, each one is about 11 inches (28 cm) in length.
* Human neck: Seven bones, too!

TECH SPECS

A giraffe's neck weighs 600 pounds (272 kg), but it stands upright by itself. An elastic ligament is always pulling the neck up, and so the giraffe only uses muscles to bring the neck down.

Thick, elastic ligament anchors the long neck to this hump on the back.

FACT FILE

Common name: Giraffe

Height: 15 ft 5 in (4.7 m)

Length: neck up to 6 ft 7 in (2 m); legs 6 ft (1.8 m); tail 3 ft 4 in (1 m)

Weight: 2.125 tons (1,930 kg)

Color: yellowy brown, with dark brown patches on body

Where it lives: open woodlands and grasslands of eastern and southern Africa

Food: leaves, twigs, fruits, and buds

Predators: lions, leopards, and hyenas

Kangaroo

The kangaroo's long feet and strange bounding body design are built for speed but also to save energy.

ENERGY RECYCLER

FACT FILE

Common name: Red kangaroo

Height: 64 in (1.6 m)

Weight: 187 lbs (85 kg)

Color: reddish fur with patches of blue-gray

Where it lives: grasslands of Australia

Food: grasses

Predators: dingoes

Long toes attached to springy fibers in leg.

Profile

The red kangaroo is a large kangaroo. There are about 60 different kinds. They are all built to hop around, which means they can cover large distances looking for plant foods and water in the dry Australian outback. The kangaroos belong to a group of mammals called marsupials, most of which live in Australia as well. Marsupial bodies have a different design than regular mammals. The female uses a pouch on her belly for carrying her babies around.

TECH SPECS

The kangaroo's springy feet bend when the animal puts its weight on them. Then they bounce back again, pushing the kangaroo into the air. This repeats with each hop, so the energy from one hop powers the next.

FAULT FINDER

Kangaroos find it hard to walk slowly in tight spaces and have to lean on their tails as they shuffle along.

Top speed: 44 mph (70 km/h)

Maximum distance: 26 ft 3 in (8 m)

JUMPING SYSTEM

TOES	Long toes work like levers, pushing the kangaroo up when the leg is straightened
TAIL	Thick, heavy tail is used for balance during hops
HEART	Heart twice the size of non-hopping mammal of the same weight
HEAD	Small so it does not overbalance the body

Polar Bear

DEEP FREEZE SURVIVOR

There are few places colder than the Arctic, but the polar bear's body is designed to survive on the frozen land and in icy water.

FACT FILE

Common name: Polar bear

Length: 8.25 ft (2.5 m)

Height: to shoulder 5 ft (1.5 m); standing upright 10 ft (3 m)

Weight: 1,100 lbs (500 kg)

Color: white-looking fur (actually clear over black skin)

Where it lives: the tundra (treeless land) and frozen ocean of the Arctic

Food: seals, fish, reindeer, seabirds, berries

Predators: other polar bears

Long hairs trap a layer of air close to the skin, which keeps the bear warm.

 BIOMIMIC:

A polar bear's hairs are hollow and have air trapped inside them. That makes the hair very good at keeping the bear warm. Some types of bedding and thick coats are filled with hollow fibers for the same reason.

Arctic temperature: -34°F (-37°C) * Freezer: 0°F (-18°C)

Profile

The polar bear is the main hunter in the Arctic. It travels long distances to find prey during the summer. In fall, conditions are too cold to hunt, and the bear hibernates under the snow all winter. It digs itself out again in spring—and is very hungry!

Hair is not white but transparent. It looks white because of the way light reflects off it.

Under skin: 4-inch (10 cm) layer of fat keeps bear warm and stores food for the winter hibernation.

COLD KILLER

The polar bear is a close relative of the brown bears that live in the forests of Asia and North America. The Arctic hunters are smaller but better adapted to life in the cold.

NOSE	Can smell prey from 20 miles (32 km) away, even through layers of ice
FEET	Soles of feet covered in hair to help grip slippery ice
STRONG SWIMMER	Can cross up to 100 miles (160 km) of ocean without stopping

Skunk

STINK SUPPLY

The small skunk's mighty defense system uses a foul smell to fend off even the largest predators.

SMELLY SQUIRTER

The skunk's smelly liquid, or musk, is made in glands inside the anus. It takes 10 days to fill a gland and that is enough for just five sprays. The skunks try to scare attackers away first, before using up their valuable musk.

HISSING	Growls and hisses with mouth
FIERCE	Stamps feet, scrapes with claws, and arches back to look larger
TAIL SIGN	Turns around and raises tail to show white underside as a final warning

Anal glands spray smelly liquid 9 feet 10 inches (3 m).

BIOMIMIC:

The smell in skunk spray comes from chemicals called thiols. Thiols are added to natural gas. They make the gas smell so people notice gas leaks.

Odor from skunk can be smelled 1 mile (1.6 km) away.

FACT FILE

Common name: Striped skunk

Length: 27 in (69 cm) including tail

Weight: 10 lbs (4.5 kg)

Color: black fur with thick white stripes on back and under tail

Where it lives: North America (other skunks live in South America)

Food: insects, mice, frogs, eggs, fruits

Predator: most hunters stay away, but eagles and owls manage to grab skunks without being spotted first

Profile

Skunks are omnivores that search for food in woodland areas. They are most active at dawn and dusk. Skunks forage by themselves using their sense of smell to find food. In cold areas, the skunks gather in groups to sleep during the day.

Tail raised when the skunk sprays.

Wide stripes on back act as a warning—making it easier to recognize the skunk!

Keen sense of smell to find food in fallen leaves.

Long claws to dig up food and burrow out a den.

Wolf

LONG JOURNEYS

Long-distance travel needs a powerful engine running inside a lightweight body. A wolf can run all night without taking a rest.

FACT FILE

Common name: Gray wolf

Length: 5 ft (1.5 m)

Weight: 110 lbs (50 kg)

Color: gray with patches of black and brown hairs

Where it lives: forests, mountains, desert, and tundra of the Northern Hemisphere, including North America, Europe, Asia, and North Africa

Prey: deer, sheep, goats, rodents, rabbits, and other small mammals

Predators: tigers in Siberia are the wolf's only natural predator

Runs at 10 mph (16 km/h) for several hours. Hits top speed of 35 mph (56 km/h) when chasing prey.

Profile

Wolves are fierce hunters. They work as a team, or pack, to kill large prey. The pack does not share food, though, so every wolf eats as quickly as possible, gulping down 20 pounds (9 kg) of meat in one meal. That's the same as 100 hamburgers!

Howls to other wolves.
Call can be heard
6 miles
(9.6 km) away.

Tongue out during
sprint to help lose
unwanted heat and
keep body cool.

Thick, muscular neck holds
large, heavy head steady
during long runs.

GOING THE DISTANCE

LEGS	Long and slender for wide strides
TOES	Short toe bones with blunt, hooked claws grip rough ground
CHEST	Big lungs fit inside wide chest to keep the body supplied with oxygen
NOSE	Long nose is lined with odor-sensitive cells to track the smells of other animals during long-distance chases

Camel

Deserts are tough places to live. The camel is built to survive the great heat, the lack of water, and the blasting sand.

DESERT SURVIVOR

FACT FILE

Common name: Dromedary camel

Length: head and body 10 ft (3 m); tail 20 in (50 cm)

Height: to shoulder 6 ft 1 in (1.85 m); to hump 7 ft 1 in (2.15 m)

Weight: 660–1,320 lbs (300–600 kg)

Color: yellowy brown, with woolly patches

Where it lives: North Africa, Middle East, and South Asia; introduced to Australia

Food: grasses and other desert plants

Hump filled with fat that provides water supply for 15 days.

 BIOMIMIC:

Skateboarders wear kneepads to cushion any falls. A camel has kneepads too. Thick layers of skin protect the knees from burning as the camel kneels on the hot sand.

Profile

There are two species of camel. The dromedary, which has one hump, lives in North Africa and the Middle East. Dromedaries have been used as pack animals for 5,000 years. Bactrian camels (right) live in Central Asia. They have two humps.

Can drink 16 gallons (60 l) of water in three minutes.

Woolly fur stops sun's heat from reaching the skin and warming the body. Becomes paler in summer to reflect heat better.

DESERT SYSTEM

EYELASH	Lashes 4 inches (10 cm) long shade the eyes from the sun and keep out grit
NOSTRILS	Close to keep sand out during sandstorms
EYELID	A third see-through eyelid wipes dirt off the eye
SWEAT	Can lose a quarter of its body weight as sweat before needing to drink

Toes spread wide to keep the feet from sinking in sand. Ground temperature: 158°F (70°C)

Bat

SEEING WITH SOUND

How do you design a flying machine that won't crash, even in the dark? Try using sounds instead of sight to navigate.

FACT FILE

Common name: Leaf-nosed bat

Length: head and body 1.6–5.3 in (4–13.5 cm)

Wingspan: 3.8–36 in (9.6–91 cm)

Weight: 0.25–7 oz (7–198 g)

Color: gray-brown or yellow with a few thick white hairs

Where it lives: Central and South America, Mexico, and Caribbean islands

Food: fruits and flying insects

Predators: owls, snakes, opossums

LISTENING FOR ECHOES

A bat finds objects in the dark by making loud calls and listening to the echoes. The system is called echolocation. The time it takes for an echo to come back tells the bat how far away an object is.

LOUD CALL	Volume of call is 140 decibels, which is louder than a rock concert
EARS	"Turn off" during the call so the animal does not deafen itself
NOSE LEAF	Flap of skin on the nose used to focus the sound of the call into a beam

Profile

There are more than 1,200 species of bat. About three-quarters of them are nocturnal and use echolocation to find their way in the dark. During the day, a bat sleeps while hanging upside down. The animal's weight pulls on its toes so that they grip even when the bat is fast asleep.

Wings made of skin stretched over long finger bones. Wings beat 17 times a second. Top flight speed: 60 mph (96 km/h)

Echo travels back to bat's large ears

High-pitched call echoes off insect prey

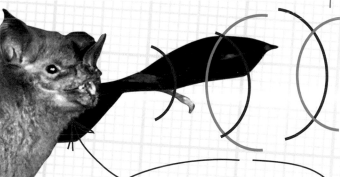

Moth

Long, pointed teeth skewer insects.

BIOMIMIC:

Sonar technology uses the same echo-bouncing system as bats. Sonar is used in submarines to show how deep the seafloor is and to pick up other subs in the water.

Elephant

SUPER STRENGTH

Equipped with a flexible trunk, lever-like tusks, and powerful body, the elephant is the animal world's answer to a bulldozer.

Profile

The African elephant is the world's largest land animal. Most live in family groups led by an older female. The family communicates using low rumbling calls that humans cannot hear. Older male elephants live by themselves.

Tail used for swatting flies on hindquarters.

BIG HITTER

SKIN	Deep wrinkles trap water and help keep the animal cool
FINGERS	Flexible tips on trunk can pick up a nut
TUSK	Used to strip bark and as a weapon
TRUNK	Sucks 3.7 gallons (14 l) of water a minute
TAIL	Tough tail used to swat flies
EARS	Enormous ears flap to release body heat

TECH SPECS

The elephant's big body is very energy efficient. It does not lose energy as quickly as smaller bodies. That allows the elephant to refuel with low-energy foods like leaves and bark.

FAULT FINDER

Despite their great feats of strength, elephants cannot jump. They are not strong enough to push their whole body off the ground.

Maximum load:
9.9 tons (9 tonnes)
* Forklift: 1 ton (907 kg)

Tusk is a long front tooth. A third of it is inside the skull. Record length: 11 ft (3.4 m)

Flexible trunk has 150,000 individual muscle blocks.

FACT FILE

Common name: African elephant

Length: head and body 16.4–24.6 ft (5–7.5 m); tail 3.25–5 ft (1–1.5 m); trunk 7 ft (2.1 m)

Height: 10–13 ft (3–4 m)

Weight: 7.5 tons (6.8 tonnes)

Color: gray-brown with wrinkled skin

Where it lives: grasslands and forests of Africa south of the Sahara Desert

Food: grasses, leaves, roots, bark, and twigs

Predators: lions, crocodiles, hyenas, and leopards attack young

Elephant is the only animal to have four knees that all bend forwards.

Sloth

TAKING IT SLOW

Want to hang out? Take a look at how the sloth does it. This animal is built for hanging from tree branches and doing nothing much at all.

FACT FILE

Common name: Sloth

Length: head and body 19–28 in (48–71 cm)

Weight: 7.7–17.6 pounds (3.5–8 kg)

Color: brown fur tinged with green

Where it lives: forests of Central and South America; stays in trees and climbs to ground only once a week

Prey: leaves, shoots, and fruit

Predator: eagle and jaguar

A tiny tail measuring 2.5 inches (6 cm) is hidden among the fur.

Tiny plantlike algae grow in the hair making it look greenish. The sloth is the only green mammal.

TECH SPECS

A sloth does not grip branches; it just hangs from 4-inch (10 cm) hooked claws. There are six species of sloth. Large species have three claws on each foot, smaller ones have two.

FAULT FINDER

Sloths have to climb down to the ground to go to the bathroom. This is a dangerous time because predators lie in wait for them.

Ground speed:
6.5 ft/min
(2 m/min)

Moves legs slowly so it does not stand out among the trees. Top speed: 13 ft/min (4 m/min)

Baby rests on mother until it is 9 months old.

Eats, sleeps, mates, and gives birth while hanging upside down.

Profile

Sloths are plant-eating forest animals. They take things slow, because that helps them stay hidden in the trees. It also helps the sloth save energy so it does not need to eat so much. The sloth's body temperature can drop to 74°F (23°C), lower than other mammals.

SLOW PROFILE

NOSE	Cannot see or hear very well and uses its nose to find food and mates
HAIR	Unlike other mammals, hairs grow up the body instead of down it
NECK	Can turn 270° from side to side, three-quarters of a full circle
SLEEP	Sloth spends almost 10 hours a day fast asleep

MECHANICALS QUIZ

Now that you know more, test your knowledge of mammals with this fun quiz. Answers on page 32.

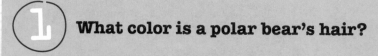 **1** What color is a polar bear's hair?

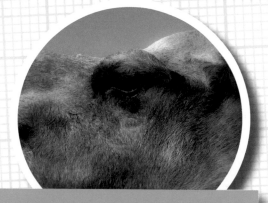

3 A human has seven bones in their neck. How many does a giraffe have in theirs?

2 How many eyelids does a camel have?

BIOMIMIC:

Elephants feel vibrations from the ground using their front foot. They lift one off the ground and concentrate on the other! The elephants are detecting vibrations made by other elephants. Scientists also measure ground vibrations to detect when earthquakes and volcanic eruptions are about to start.

4 A sloth has green fur. Which other mammals are green?

5 Chemicals like those in skunk spray are added to natural gas. Why?

MAMMAL RECORDS

BIGGEST	Blue whale 110 ft (34 m); 200 tons (181,000 kg)
SMALLEST	Etruscan shrew 1.6 in (4 cm); 0.063 oz (1.8 g)
FASTEST	Cheetah 70 mph (113 km/h)
SLOWEST	Sloth 0.16 mph (0.25 km/h)
TALLEST	Giraffe 15 ft 5 in (4.7 m)
STRONGEST	Elephant, lifts 10 tons (9 tonnes)
LONGEST LIFE	Bowhead whale 211 years
HOTTEST	Camel body temperature 107°F (42°C)
COLDEST	Sloth body temperature 74°F (23°C)

Glossary

aerodynamic Shaped to allow air to flow around it easily without causing any blockages.

algae Microscopic plantlike organisms that use photosynthesis to make food.

anal To do with the anus, the rear opening of the digestive system.

Arctic The region around the North Pole. Most of the Arctic is covered by a frozen ocean.

cells The tiny building blocks of a living body.

circulate To send around in a circle or loop. Blood circulates around a body, carrying oxygen and food supplies.

component A part of a larger unit.

decibel The unit used to measure the volume of sound. A normal conversation is 60 decibels.

forage To look for food.

hibernate To become sleepy and inactive during the winter.

ligament A tough cord that connects bones together at joints.

mammal A group of animals that have hair and feed their young with milk.

marsupial A type of mammal that carries its young inside a pouch.

musk A powerful smell produced by an animal. Musk is used to scare away predators and to attract mates.

nocturnal To be active during the night when it is dark.

odor A smell.

omnivore An animal that eats both plants and animals. "Omni" means all, while "vore" means eater.

oxygen The gas taken from the air by the lungs that is used inside the body to release energy.

predator An animal that hunts other animals for food.

pressure A measure of how much force is concentrated into an area.

prey An animal that is hunted by another animal.

sonar A detection system that uses sounds and echoes.

thiol A chemical containing carbon, sulfur, and hydrogen. Most thiols smell very bad.

transparent See-through.

tundra Land that is frozen for most of the year. Only grasses and small plants grow there.

Further Information

Books

Beaumont, Holly. *Why Do Monkeys and Other Mammals Have Fur?* Chicago, IL: Heinemann Raintree, 2016.

Levine, Sara. *Bone by Bone: Comparing Animal Skeletons.* Minneapolis, MN: Millbrook Press, 2014.

Levine, Sara. *Tooth by Tooth: Comparing Fangs, Tusks, and Chompers.* Minneapolis, MN: Millbrook Press, 2016.

Lewis, Clare. *Mammal Body Parts.* Chicago, IL: Heinemann Raintree, 2016.

Rajczak, Kristen. *20 Fun Facts about Mammal Adaptations.* New York: Gareth Stevens Publishing, 2016.

Spilsbury, Louise. *What Is the Structure of an Animal?* New York: Britannica Educational Publishing, 2014.

Websites

PowerKids Press has developed an online list of websites related to the subject of this book. This site is updated regularly. Please use this link to access the list:

www.powerkidslinks.com/am/mammals

Index

Answers to the Quiz:

1. See-through, the hairs contain no color
2. Three; one eyelid is see-through
3. Seven
4. None, the sloth is the only green mammal
5. The smell alerts people to gas leaks